Moods

Emotional Diary Through Poetry

by

Irina M. Creaser

DORRANCE PUBLISHING CO., INC.
PITTSBURGH, PENNSYLVANIA 15222

with deep appreciation and thanks
to my mother who has been my friend
through all the difficult times of my life

ISBN # 0-8059-3829-X
Printed in the United States of America

First Printing

For more information or to order additional books, please write:
Dorrance Publishing Co., Inc.
643 Smithfield Street
Pittsburgh, Pennsylvania 15222
U.S.A.

CONTENTS

Shadow Of My Mind

When the sun lights the sky
a shadow grows tall
you can't touch it, can't hold it
you can't catch it at all.

Then the moon lights the night
and my shadow stands high
I know I can't catch it
yet I try, yes I try

And then comes the time
when there's no light at all
and your shadow is gone
I had no chance at all

There is a fire in my heart
burning deep, burning bright
burning longer and stronger
than any known light

It brings back your shadow
forever, in my mind
where ever my thoughts go
your shadow they'll find

Your memory is in me
to never forget
I thrill when I see you
the pains I don't regret

You are that shadow
most elusive of all
you are questions, not answers
and you leave with nightfall

Your eyes are mysterious
they smolder like coal
they burn deep in my heart
they are searching my soul.

My mind is your captive
you are haunting my dreams
you play games with my feelings
with your sorcery and schemes

My pain is your pleasure
my suffering your goal
the love that I gave you
is taking it's toll

Shadow of my mind
temptation of my heart
I will never find peace
yet hope never to part.

I am a victim
of passion and hate
I do not seek rescue
it is long time too late

2. *Only The Shadow Knows*

Last night I saw your shadow
though my eyes were closed
when will I see you once again
only the shadow knows

Once we'd talked, you said to me
'only the shadow knows'
the answer how, and where and when
to be or not to be

That night my heart was filled with joy
I knew my love was true
how do I tell him, words are cheap
I wish my shadow knew

Oh, does he know, he fills my life
each night with dreams a-new
that every day my joyful heart
beats longingly for you.

Oh, does he know how high the price
the pain of love can be
and that I pay a thousand fold
for every smile at me

The choice is yours
wherever we'll go
if our lips will ever meet
only the shadow'll know

My love will never fade away
I always will be true
and when I'm dust and gone for good
know - I lived just for you

From then on to eternity
I'll be a shadow, too
and when two shadows merge as one
they will be me and you.

3. *Lonesome Thoughts Of You*

A tear softly drops
from the corner of my eye
the way it takes many have taken
each time that I cry

It's not easy to laugh
when your heart cries in pain
to smile and go on
when I love you in vain

You know, my love, I search for you
in all these secret places
where you and me had met and kissed
where we shared sweet embraces

Like the evening star
with it's beautiful light
it is so far away
yet is shining so bright

This star and it's light forever are there
though, there are times when you cannot see
it's like the love in my heart
which I hold there for thee.

4. *Painful Nights Of Shadows*

In the still of the night
I hear my heart softly break
a choice I have made
a pain gladly I take

The dark of the night
heals the pain of the lonely
but it never can still
my tears cried for you only

There is more to the night
than anyone knows
that when I dream of your shadow
my pain steadily grows

Fool, that I am
to give my heartblood for you
I try holding a shadow
which will never be true

Now I am past healing
my tears all are dry
you are part of my soul now
to forget, I must die.

5. *A Heart Of Love*

If you like the full moon
I will bring it to you
to show you my love
which will always be true

If you want the stars
you just have to command
I will reach for them all
to lay in your hand

If my pain brings you joy
just let me know
I will tear out my heart
I will let my blood flow

But all that I offer
means nothing to you
it's just my heart full of love
without that you can do

6. Teardrop - Song For A Shadow

A heart full of love
to you to belong
it beats only for you
but longtime you're gone

The day that I met you
brought pain I've never known
you left me hoping and wanting
you gave me a dream, but I'm dreaming alone

The moments you're with me
are just in my mind
where between longing and pain
your sweet memory I find

Oh, come to me - shadow
when you hear my heart call
it's song 's made of teardrops
dreaming of you they do fall.

7. *Silent Torment*

So different are the two I love
and yet I feel the same
three lives are joined with sacred bond
and I'm the one to blame

My heart, why does your joyfull beat
have such a saddened sound?
it is the love I feel for one
and knowing that I'm bound

There are these little lies I tell
to save my wandering heart
and knowing I betray one's love
is tearing me apart

One heart to give - two men to love
and no choice can be made
whom will I loose - whom will I win
the answer is my fate.

One who had claimed me long ago
with name and wedding band
I gave my faithfulness and love
together with my hand

I'll never loose his love and care
but I know I need more
it is your passion and your warmth
I've never felt before

The secret love I hold for you
consumes me with a passion
and when my heart aches silently
I long to make confession

The torments of my mind invade my dreams
each time I try to sleep
they are the battles of my heart
which rage within me deep.

If forsaking you 's the only way
to rescue my torn soul
like tearing out my very heart
it's much too high a toll.

I'd rather give up peace of mind
each time I think of you
it is the sweetest dream of love
which never will come true

3. *Magical Dreams*

You are as elusive as moondust
that falls golden on the first night of May
you are as rare and as hard to find
as the one famous needle in a stack of hay

You are as precious as a four-leaf of clover
that makes all my wishes come true
and I'm wishing for that rainbow over my shoulder
which is the only way to you

Your smile is as bright as the brightest of stars
that I see in a dark summer night
your eyes are as deep as the deepest of oceans
where there never will be any light

Your promises fade like the dew in the morning
when the sun will rise at dawn
you are the most wonderful dream, I have dreamt
but when I open my eyes, you are gone

If all the fairies and mysteries come true
a dreamer is what I would be
and I'd escape to that magical land
where forever I would be with thee.

9. *Stranger In My Dreams*

My body lies asleep at night
and yet my mind 's aware
of one dark stranger in my heart
a man for whom I care

Dark stranger you have come to me
in every sleepless night
invading dream and peace of mind
come morning you take flight

Tall stranger let me see your face
and let me hear your voice
so that I know my sleepless nights
are not a curse by choice

Mysterious stranger, please don't go
and leave me in despair
will you for once just soothe my pain
and tell me that you care

My stranger with the velvet eyes
please, smile once more for me
and kiss away the tears I cried
when I am not with thee.

0. *In Absence Of You*

Bereft I am of all I had
your absence leaves me shattered
your smile, your touch and tender kiss
is all that ever mattered.

For all the storms we weathered pale
against my dying heart
and that I'm but a hollow shell
since the moment, we did part

I know, my smile has lost it's warmth
my eyes have lost their shine
until the moment, you will call me
mine, forever mine.

But until then my life will be
a night without an end
until you come and claim what's your's
with golden wedding band

And you know that I pledge my love
and that my heart be true
and that I wait without an end
to have a life with you.

11. Weathered Storms

We've braved and weathered every storm
that fate had thrown our way
but now we must be stronger yet
to face each lonely day

In screaming silence I am lost
to seek a dream of you
to have you fill my very life
with tender love from you

My body trembles with the loss
of not to have you near
so let your memory soothe my mind
and take away my tears

Let me draw strength from every breath
from every smile you give
So I won't falter in despair
'cause for you I have to live

Come, rescue me and stop the fears
which every night I cry
for happiness will only come
while in your arms I lie.

2. A Fool's Dream

A penny of copper
a bullet of lead
a heart full of love
is all that I had

All that I would offer
to you on my knees
but you laughed in my face
and denied me my pleas

Each night I would dream
that your heart turned my way
and I named you my hero
like in a play

There's a knight in his armor
that fights for his queen
a mysterious gypsy
that plays tambourine

A dark-hooded stranger
when I'm in distress
and my tall, handsome Indian
to bring happiness.

But the real you is different
deceiving and cruel
and you laugh at the dreams
of a loving - you fool.

You can call me a fool
since I know what you are
'cause I can't stop to love you
not by far - not by far.

And I'll continue to see you
the way only I can
as a fool's lonesome dream
of a shadow - not a man.

13. *Universe Of Love*

Over hills into the mountains
where the air is fresh and clear
where the sunbeams are so close to touch
that's where I feel you near

Through the rapids of the rivers
into the deep blue sea
where the sky and ocean meet as one
that's were I'll wait for thee

You make me feel the universe
the earth's living core
the moving of the ocean's tides
from shore to endless shore

You woke me up from dreamless sleep
to lift me to the sky
where I will soar, the sun as guide
and you're the reason why

I do not know, what lies beyond
the dreams which we do share
but I am not afraid with you
to find out, what waits there

Let happiness be our goal
and let love see us through
be tenderness and trust our way
to start each day a-new.

4. Why All?

Why has every dream I've had
shattered and broken in two
my heart hurts so and I feel dead
I know that I've lost you

Why, why have all that I helt dear
left me - to fall apart
to loose a dream I never dreamt
and die with a broken heart

Why can my eyes not focus straight
without my tears to fall
why have I hurt all that I loved
I loved, I lost - why all

15. Lost, Alone And Gone

My tears have just now stopped to flow
but have I ceased to love
my pain will never go away
as long as there are stars above.

The hurting has just now begun
in an unending, relentless way
for I pay dearly and unmercilessly
for every unfaithful day.

Your voice and your smile are haunting me
your eyes keep me sleepless at night
peace and salvation is all that I seek
but to whom will I turn in my plight.

Can my life be mended can I be saved
the answer I do not know
I aimlessly wander, lost and alone
afraid, with no place to go.

The fear of tomorrow makes me shake in despair
I tremble with pain in my heart
such emotions of sorrow I never have known
but with you in my life they did start

I grasped for a dream, believing it true
a rainbow I thought I could hold
the shadow of your smile I took as my sun
to find out that it's light had no warmth and was cold

I realize all and bend my head
my spirit has been broken
my tormented heart seeks final rest
but no comfort has been spoken

There are no arms to take me in
no shoulder on which to lie
no words to soothe and dry my tears
and no one to will weep when I die.

Let earth then open and swallow me whole
for that is where I belong
no one will miss me, I brought nothing but pain
please, forgive me for all I've done wrong.

And yet let me thank you for a love I thought mine
a feeling, so tender and new
a heart filled with passion, a storm through my life
that only through you could come true

Forget me, darling, for I am but a dream
remember the good things we shared
wake up to a new life that won't know who I am
just a memory that always will care.

16. *New Beginnings*

Now, that I've closed the book of life
the chapter of my troubled past
will I wake up to bright tomorrows
and will forever my love last?

Now, that I've left the road of turmoil
of pains, that left me hurt and weak
will I find peace forever after
and the forgiveness that I seek?

Now, that my mind is clear and focused
I see the mistakes that I have made
I try to erase from my memory
the things I've done, but it's too late.

Is it too late to start all over?
I ask you humbly on my knees
can you forget the pain I've caused you
will you accept my love and pleas?

Then hold me close to hear your heartbeat
and kiss away the tears I cry
now, let's forget and love each other
and give our life another try.

7. *Most Precious Tears*

Precious tears have long collected
in strong man's tender heart
from your pains and from the anguish
that you've vowed I'd never see.
one more time I felt your hurting
and I took you in my arms
and I touched your moistened lashes
with a kiss I set you free,

Then the moon caressed you gently
where silver tears had drawn their way
this was a different man, there laying,
one, whose heart was not of stone
once you were not ashamed of crying
you shed these teardrops one by one

You looked so peaceful while I soothed you
we didn't speak to break the magic
while crying in my arms you lay
these precious tears are your way saying:
"I love you more than manly pride;
you've seen a 'me', none knew existed
a part of me I used to hide."

And when my heart is close to breaking
and there be teardrops in my eyes
kiss them away and hold me gently
while I am resting on your bosom
quivering with unmanly cries.

18. Talk From Mind To Heart

"Hello, my heart, how are you feeling
you pound so strong within me deep."
"I pump your blood, I keep you living
I rise with every breath you take."
"I also hold your inner secrets
I feel your pain, know when you weep
I skip a beat when you are happy
only to hurt and nearly break"

"Say, heart do you feel different at day or night,
asleep or when I'm wide awake?"
"Not really, mind, 'cause you stay active
you think about the good and bad.
I never rest, my beat is steady
while I am wondering what plans you make
but no one knows, I'm often crying
and bleed because I know you're sad."

"Why bother, heart, what I am thinking
a mind has naught to do with you."
"Wish, you were right, but it is different,
have you not thought, that we are one?
When you think thoughts of love, I'm racing
when I am still, you feel pain, too,
and when at last I will stop beating
forever me and you are gone."

9. *Rivers Of Tears*

How deep are the rivers of tears that I've cried
while you thought that I felt no pain
and no one heard my silent screams
when I begged for your love in vain.

How much more can I hurt before my heart breaks
when will my last teardrop fall to the ground?
Will the silver lines, they have drawn, ever dry
will I be happy with the love I've found?

When will my dark nights turn into daylight
when do I stop running, to face the world brave and strong
when will all dreams, that I dream, have happy endings
when do I finally feel I belong?

When will the rivers of tears stop flowing
and when will the oceans, they have filled, dry?
When will my heart of glass cease it's breaking
with every tear drop that falls, when I cry?

When will all questions, I've asked, be answered
when will I forget how it is, to be sad?
Will I find happiness and love, while I'm living
or wait for peace and fulfillment until I'm dead.

20. *Last Request*

How lost and how alone an aching heart can be
when carelessly cast to the ground
when tears and blood are flowing free
and love nowhere can be found.

Now tears are streaming unhelt to the floor
and consciousness 's slipping away
my breathing is ceasing till I am no more
and there still forever I lay

Now above my body my soul 's floating high
to see if someone would care
but all I had known, had wished me to die
there is no one to weep, I am sadly aware

My peaceful remains lay cold while they wait
for a grave that will have no stone
forever forgotten will be my fate
my life had been short, unloved, lost, and alone

But one last request I ask to make
that the one who had caused me pain
through my memory I will his heart to instantly break
and for eternity it shall so remain.

1. ***Dreamland***

Drift to sleep my tired body
float away my tortured mind
to a secret place in heaven
where no mortal soul you'd find

Where the unicorns and dragons
of your storybook run free
and the fairy prince and princess
live in perfect harmony

It's a world just known to dreamers
where all fairytales come true
where the man you'd always dreamt of
tenderly loves none but you.

Dreamland has one purpose only
to ease your heart and still your tears
it brightens up your bleak tomorrows
and takes away your dreadfull fears

A handsome pirate takes you captive
but gives his love to you instead
a magic prince will make you princess
and puts a crown up on your head

Where strong knights rescuing fair maidens
and mermaids give up life for love
where gods and goddesses are living
up on Olympus, high above

It's where are rainbows never ending
and sirens sing their luring song
a place of mystery and wonders
where only dreamers do belong.

Not many have imagination
it is an art of very few
but every time my heart starts breaking
I withdraw to dreamland once anew

22. *Minstrel's Song*

A minstrel came to my castle long ago
to seek entrance and I let him in
he had nothing to pay for room and board
but the songs that he offered to sing

I asked him: come closer while I sat on my throne
and he laid on the floor near my feet
he said "Forgive me M'Lady, for what I'm to say
but it's a lovesong I know that you need."

I smiled at him sadly 'cause I knew he was right
last night's tears were just barely dry
could the minstrel, a stranger, have known my despair
and more, would he also know why?

I asked him to sing and he bowed his head
then he took out his harp, and he started to play
I could not help but wonder what he was to sing
then his voice touched my heart in a mysterious way

His voice was clearer than church bells
and as fresh as the dew
he sang a song of my life
and of my tears about you

He sang of a fair lady who had given her love
to a man who had conquered her heart
she was blinded by hope that his promise come true
then he hurt her and used her till she fell apart

The bard sang of her hardships, her tears, and her pain
that her lover was violent and she shuddered in fear
but the wish, she could hate him and leave him
faded fast, when his arm held her near.

T'was no ord'nary minstrel 'cause he knew far too much
his song had scared me for all had come true
the last verse was my future, what was it to be
would we stay together or would I soon be without you?

I begged him to stop and not sing the end
and he bowed and he smiled knowingly
soon my life will be one dark lonely road
with his song my only memory of thee

Now the minstrel is gone, I never saw him again
my grand castle has faded away
and I am no princess, or lady of rank
just a lonesome sad woman, dreaming of a happier day.

3. *Over The Edge*

I can feel my tears run salty lanes
across an empty face
and eyes not seeing dark or light
just staring into space.

My heart of glass has shattered to pieces
my card-house has fallen apart
I've fallen into an endless pit
please, someone, I need a new start!

Am I alone while I cry for help
is there no-one to listen to me
where have my friends gone when I need them most?
They vanished, conveniently

All who had loved me
through laughter and cheers
forgot me
at first sight of tears

A memory is all that I have left
of songs which are fading fast
and I close my eyes to dream away
of an imaginary past.

I hear the sounds of an echo repeating my tears
and the four walls around are the friends listening to me
and my cats are the only ones showing concern
for my deep melancholy

I feel so homeless with my wandering heart
and I know not which road I should take
am I lost in a circle with no place to go
no way out till my spirit will break?

The end is to lose my sanity and mind
to lose the feeling if I'm loved or not
to no more see, nor hear, or feel
and finally forgotten by this earthly lot.

24. In Another Time

Another time - another place
with dreams not so untouchable high
I wish that I could simply fly
just like a bird but without wings
I'm dreaming of impossible things

As my eyes close I ramble on
and talk of things so long-time gone
I see a girl smile happily
she never knew what tears would be
and as the pages turn and turn
I see the girl change into me
sad and crying suddenly.

How I have changed from then to now
oh, how I wish I'd known
I would have never planned for this
oh, say, why have I grown?

I wish to turn the page of time
and try once more anew
I would re-do all that I have done
and never be with you.

My eyes are like the deep green sea
but always at high tide
they shine and sparkle with tears from within
and their steady flow I can't hide

You've taught me pain and how to cry
more than I wanted to know.
It's time these tears are drying up
and we both know I should go.
Another time - another place
we will do well -- I know.

5. *What Is Love*

Each one of us had asked one day:
what does the word "love" mean.
how to define, how to describe?
impossible it does seem.

And no philosopher I am
yet this I'd like to tell:
where scholars wonder what is love
I know the answer well.

So let me share my wisdom now
for what I say is true
that love 's a many splendor thing
but most of all: it's you.

It is the way you make me feel
so endlessly fulfilled
to know you are the solid rock
on which we both can build.

It is the sparkle in your eyes
the way you smile at me
the way you gently hold my hand
and kiss me tenderly

It is the way I know your thoughts
before you speak your mind
it is the passion we both feel
and nowhere else could find

It is the way you make me laugh
the way I care for you
it's all the little things we share
and everything we do.

It also is the tears I cry
emotions high and low
the way you hold me close to you
and never let me go.

It's anger, pain, and happiness
the need to have you near,
it's trust, and joy, and childish glee
shared worries, doubts, and fear.

You are all that fulfills my life
what God sent from above
my dreams all start and end with you
you are the meaning "love".

26. *Confession Of Love*

We have no lesser quarrels
than other couples do
except at all our endings
the more that I love you

I've never claimed I'm perfect
and surely never be
so more that I appreciate
that a man like you loves me.

I am a better person
since you took over reign
thanks to your love and caring
I'll never be the same

You've taught me all your values
and broadened up my mind
if all my life I'd searched this world
no greater man I'd find.

Your strength in heart and mind and soul
still make me gaze at you
with admiration in my eyes
while saying I love you.

So at the end I'm asking
no more than I can give
which means: let's go on loving
as long as we both shall live.

7. *The Curse*

No one had touched my life like you
no one had set my heart aflame
with passion - no one else could tame.

While when you hold me tenderly
I feel love of infinity
to just belong to only one
whom God alone would not condone.

And while I pray He'd change his mind
the sands of time have past away
and where once in your arms I'd lay
another woman holds my place
and gently you will kiss her face
I envy her the love she'll find.

Is my fate one of loneliness,
a life where love will be a-miss!?
No, no I scream
this all was just a horrid dream

My lover loves no one but me
he waits for me eternally
and I do not need to despair
because his strong arms will be there
to hold forever my life and heart
until the day God makes us part.

There not again be love like this
to hold two lives with such strong bond
to give two hearts such sinful bliss
we have been chosen to feel feelings beyond
anything that's known as happiness.

But know this - there is but one way
to make our love come true
for you there can be none but me
and for me no one but you.

We have been blessed and cursed in one
we never will be free
you are to love but me alone
all else will leave you cold.
And I too, will be without love
until I'm joined by thee.

28. *The Hammock*

There she's laying in her hammock
thinking of the two years past
of the dreams made in this hammock
of a love she thought would last

Faded are the hammock's colors
and those dreams have faded too
no one knows she's broken-hearted
'cause her love will not come true

The murmor from the rustling leaves
is like a love-song so long past
when two lips kissed - two hearts were beating
a wild tattoo she thought would last

Her heart now beats so faint and mournful
her parched lips thirsting for a kiss
her trembling body longs to drown
in his embrace - such sinful bliss

There she is swinging in her hammock
the scent of fresh grass in the air
her eyes are closed while she smiles gently
she's lost in dreams and thinks he's there.

9. Long Ago-Yesterday

When long ago I fell in love
the world was not to know
the truth was mine alone to keep
and not to tell a soul
but this was long ago

I loved you near - I loved you far
but in a silent way
I could not sing my happiness
Your name was not to leave my lips
but this was yesterday

Then suddenly our lives had changed
and all the world could know
that love was our's - for all to see
that no more we would have to hide
like we did long ago

But then life struck a sudden blow
the pain still makes me sway
our hearts were torn and scattered far
that never more we'll find our love
for now and ev'ry day

30. *Poet In The Sky*

The roaring engine is my music
and through my window is the sky
I feel that I could reach and touch
the cotton clouds - if I just try

The world looks small, so microscopic
a multicolored carpet piece
and I describe - not philosophic
the tiny houses, streams and trees

The scene has changed
and clouds are forming gigantic castles in the air
and we could reach them - all we must do...
...is walk the rainbow - if we dare

31. Depressions

Depression, invader of the mind
unfortold and silently
a panther that will stalk his prey
his kill swift and efficiently

Such is depression - undetected
until it settles like a veil
all thoughts turn bleak no hope in sight
a ship without a sail

Like quicksand, slowly closing in
no one to pull you out
an endless desert without rain
a voice without a loud.

Such overbearing obstacle
can there be victory
for in the end it's do or die
to be or not to be

How do I win the fight atlast
to be depression-free
it is a battle of my wills
and thoughts of blissful glee.

32. *Happiness*

Be happy with what you got and don't complain
with every bit of sunshine there has to be rain
think of some one who has less when you want more
and that happiness is always just a step from your door

There is always someone out there who needs a helping hand
and when you have a problem, one will understand.
A smile can be so much more than you could ever give
So go smiling through the world just as long as you live

There are good sides and bad sides to all things
and no one knows exactly what tomorrow brings.
Have faith, be kind, and always do you best
and the good Lord above, He will work on the rest.

33. *Without You*

What are you doing to my heart
what have you done, where did it go
I felt it break not long ago
now emptiness is tearing me apart

I do not ask you: give it back
just give me your heart in return
it is your love, your tenderness
for which I've come to yearn

Within me burns a wanton need
to fill my one desire
which is to love you and be loved
and feed our passion's fire.

What magic have you used on me
I think of none but you
I do not care 'bout nothing else
as long as your love is true

I hear your voice, I see your smile
thoughts of you make me sing
sweet pain of longing fills my heart
love is a wonderous thing.

34. *Rambling Thoughts*

He just stopped loving me today
he changed his mind and walked away
I don't know why my heart is breaking
am I to cry? - I feel so taken

I had been warned of my mistake
but 't was a chance I had to take
gone are the fantasies and all the dreams,
I just awoke and nothing's as it seems.

Reality has a life of it's own
and when you awake you will be all alone.

5. *Toy Love*

I'm like a toy
and all toys get discarded
when they are nomore new
and no more fun to play.
Now it's my turn,
my newness gone, the thrill 's worn off.
Soon I will find a place where I'll will put away.

I'll be forgotten
except for memories that I served my purpose well
and in his mind he'll think
that I was fun to have around
but not enough to be forever bound.
That he was wrong only time can tell.

36. True Feelings

It's good to have someone like you
to love and to hold tight
to hug and kiss and cuddle on
and go to sleep each night

Each precious moment that we share
feels twice as good with you
and knowing when you say you care
you really mean, you do

To know I'm loved inspite of all
is more than I could ask
since difficult I often am
it's not an easy task

You give me strength to make each day
a reason to go on
it is through your sweet loving way
that I feel I belong

You are so special that I think
that I deserve you not
and yet I hope I'm good enough
for you is all I've got

For all the world I could not tell
how much I love you, Sweet -
so I just wrote this little note
and hope it's all you need

37. *Through The Seasons*

The summer 's past
and slowly fall has settled in
to paint with orange red and yellow
our leaves - to cover up the green

The days grow shorter now
and soon the sun-rays won't be warm but cold
the flocks of birds are flying south
and soon all trees will wear a coat of gold

Now it is time for Halloween and pumpkin-pie
the harvest of the fields was longtime taken in
Thanksgiving with the scent of turkeys fills the air
and folks are sitting round the fires with their kin

The trees have lost all leaves by now
so sad and empty look their mighty crowns
but they're just waiting for the winter season to begin
and there'll be dressed in flaky snow white gowns

Warm coats and gloves are worn again
and booted feet tread over hardened ground
the mornings are now dark and often cold
and 'round the windows signs of early frost are found

The children's carols ringing through the crisp cool air
and icicles are glistening in the winter sun
the frozen lake looks like a mirror where skaters waltzing merrily
the snowball fights are fought with laughter
and sleighing down the hill is so much fun

Chestnuts are roasting in the fire
baked apples are most well-liked treats
the yule-log burns and Christmas trees are decorated
the lists for Santa are all written
and busy shoppers hurry through the streets

We wish this season lasts forever, for all is peaceful yet so merry
and all the world seems to be dressed in white
but soon the snow will melt and our days be longer
while nights and darkness will be chased by light

The soggy grounds are ready for their springtime planting
and fresh green buds are to be seen on ev'ry tree
the birds return and soon will start their nesting
and Easter-egg-hunts are so filled with glee

It seems from one day to another
the world has turned all shades of green
the spring was quick replaced by summer
and bikes and tennis players can be seen.

The summer sun is shining brightly
so BBQ's and picnics are just the thing to do
and to cool off the people are seen jumping
into a river or a lake of blue

Amusement parks are open daily
and schools are closing for the summer break
enjoy your tan, the heat and sun of this great season
for soon we will have come full circle and
season fall will follow summer's wake

8. Commitment For The Future

I'm living for lovin'
and I'm lovin' my living
but you know you get nothing
without doing some giving

So give me the love
that I gave from my heart
let's hold on to each other
now that we've got a new start

Let the past be the past
the future lays bright ahead
now we got something
which before we never had

39. *Before I Sleep*

Please Lord, forgive me for the things I have done
I know I should remorse but I really feel none
I need his love more than I could ever tell
please, Lord, forgive me and don't send me to hell

Please, Lord, understand that he's all I need
that when I'm with him I fell so complete
that my life would be empty if not for his kiss
please, Lord, understand I just could not resist.

Please, Lord, understand since you know me best
to love and be loved is your greatest test
to bring us together must have been your plan
Lord, I hope I am right and you sent me this man

Lord, it feels so good to know you're there for me
that with all my feelings I can turn on to Thee
so I want to thank you in the heavens above
for fulfilling my life with this man and his love

Lord, I could never tell what his love means to me
that he makes me happy the way I thought could not be
that his very nearness makes me feel so secure
Lord, I never knew love like this, honest and pure

Lord, just one last thought before I go to sleep
the love that we share I forever would keep
and if you could grant us this bliss to last
being unloved and lonely be a thing of the past

And, Lord, please, protect him and watch ov'r him for me
'cause without his love I just don't want to be
you already know that I need him so
and that unless you take him I won't let him go.

0. ***The Bird Of Death***

Lies lies lies - you lied to me while you were saying
the words which I had longed to hear
I love you, baby, you had said, until the day I die
I'll never leave you, give you up, I'll never say good-bye
and yet, while happy in your arms, I could not shake the fear
the premonition which I had - proved much to right one day.

You broke my heart with one swift word, deep to my deepest core
I love you baby - I must leave and see you never more
Oh cruel, so cruel my fate has been
to give and take away
to make me feel so cherished by one whom I adore
and then one day just perished and hurt like nev'r before

Your love is now an open wound
a switch blade aimed to kill
I was naught but an episode
to love and leave at will

And sightless I stare at the ceiling
collect my thoughts before I sleep
and yet my mind is constant drifting
to the raven who had made me weep.

I had a dream once of a bird - a raven I recall
he was so strong - I loved him so his wings a shield to me
He cared for me, protected me but then he let me fall
my dream came true, my pain is real - the raven, it was thee.

Raven, Raven, bird of death,
why have you come calling
will you bring pain or happiness,
save me before I'm falling.

41. *Premonition*

It was not midnight while I pondered
't was daylight that I sat and wondered
about a bird I saw while sleeping
a raven, which had made me weeping

It was an omen sent to warn me
about a man who soon would scorn me
first he would love me like no other
but then his error he'd discover

That he had given much to ready
his heart which did not beat too steady
and soon his love would fade away
like memories of yesterday

Yes we were meant to be together
that we were soul-mates now and ever
I've known this from the very start
but did not know he'd break my heart

42. *The Prize Of Love*

Eyes open seeing yet not seeing
tears running, I'm running, yes I'm fleeing
to seek a little peace of mind
for all the despair which I find

Pain like a dagger in my heart
apart from you - together yet apart
and shadows overcast my days
such are love's ways

I am a drifter
without hope
my life is running through a sifter
I don't know how to cope

Love is bitter
love is pain
you're up - you're down
what is your gain?

43. Getting Over You

There's just no getting over you
no matter what I do
a million miles will never do
in getting over you

I could set world records
win trophies one or two
but all the fame and fortune
won't get me over you

At last I'll drown my broken heart
in an ocean deep and blue
but even death won't break us up
'cause my soul will be with you

44. My Estate

When finally my light goes out
and all is dark and still
then you'll know what I've talked about
when they'll read my last will

To the world I'll leave my laughter
'cause they need all of it
I know that there is so much hurt
which laughter could defeat.

My heart I don't know whom to give
'cause it caused naught but pain
it is a worthless treasure
with naught but tears to gain.

Ah, yes, who'll keep my silvry tears
their flow has still not dried
much wealth they promise with their salt
for oceans I have cried

And finally I leave my love
which slowly did me in
'cause in my quest for happiness
my love turned into sin

Who'd want this cursed love of mine
just bury it with me
for in the end my love was none
but murder first degree

This is my will and testament
now I can go to sleep
the world is better without me
my estate no one will keep.

45. Secret Room

I just have closed a special room
which once held me and you
in this room I have also locked
my dreams which won't come true

There also is a secret room
within this heart of mine
which keeps all thoughts and memories
of you, my love divine.

My dreams have just turned into ashes
a fire blazing once so high
was naught but straw and fast is dying
and with these flames I too will die.

46. *The Last Good-Bye*

My baby just left me
'cause I told her so
she walked out of my life
'cause I told her to go

So many times
have I sent her away
so sure of myself
that I knew she would stay

But today she just walked
when I turned her loose
she left me for good
'cause I made her choose

When she stopped and she turned
there were tears in her eyes
with a sad smile she said
"this is my last good-bye"

I was your daytime mistress
with heartaches at night
'cause you would not hold me
when daylight took flight

My heart, body and soul
I had given to thee
but you could not decide
to leave her or keep me

A convenience and thrill
I have been in your life
to love and be loved
but not as your wife

I cannot live
with fear of every tomorrow
what would it bring?
laughter or sorrow

I don't count the price
of this love for you
all I had wanted
was to make dreams come true

There is nothing else
which I know to do
I just cannot live
with the anger in you

I am afraid
for each word that I say
and I worry and wonder
when will you cast me away

To say good-bye
always hurts that is true
now I'm saying my last
good-bye to you

My memories and love for you
I'll take to my grave
may you find what you searched for
good bye, darling RAVE.

47. *Dying Dreams*

How sad and lonesome
a shattered broken heart can be
when all you hear 's the haunting echo
of it's joyfull beating melody

This heart was given much too freely
then, used and cast onto the ground
where now in thousand little pieces
my once so happy heart is found

In an unmarked gravesite there lay buried
my dreams which died the same day too
they had been crushed by careless hands while carried
by the man they were entrusted to

The pain I feel and all my mourning
is not for dreams which did just die
it's for a love which lives within me
and won't be answered - I do cry.

I now must live on mem'ries only
of days when you had filled my past
my love for you will go on burning
till the day when I will die at last

I know forever, I will love you
and dream of plans which we did make
I cry when thinking of that future
we'd built together - you did forsake.

48. *Dying Fire*

Watch the fire, fire, fire
as the flames grow high and higher
as the red and blue and yellow
make you feel so warm and mellow

How the heat goes to your soul
as the wood turns into coal
there is promise, there is hope
as you watch the flames and cope

Mesmerizing, dancing, motion
make you dream of love-devotion
fantasizing, thinking, dreaming
while in the fire there lies gleaming
a broken heart that now is dying
and silver tears which I've been crying

Too soon the flames are growing colder
they nomore leap and dance and smolder
and like a love that had been killed
the fire also has been stilled
the sole remains of this hot fire
are memories, dreams but no desire

49. *Searching For Love*

If I were a rose
in your garden I'd grow
for you'll treat me with care
this much I do know

If I'd be a bird
I would nest in your tree
where I feel cherished and safe
protected by thee

But I'm not a bird
or a rose growing free
just a woman needing love
calling for thee.

Take my heart, treat it gently
'cause it scars much too fast
it needs a safe keeping
and a love that would last.

I've been broken and crashed
like the petals of a rose
I've paid long enough
for the wrong road I'd chose

Now I'm starting all over
with you in my mind
and I hope and I pray
that true love we'll find

I do know that you're special
that you're gentle and kind
I can trust in your strength
both in body and mind

And no matter what -
I can depend on you too
you are honest and caring
with a heart that is true

And you, just like me
need to receive and give love
fill each other's void
giving more than enough.

50. *Magic of Love*

Raindrops falling on the window
and my teardrops falling too
as the angels cry in heaven
I am crying here for you.

For there are many miles between us
and I am so alone at night
I dream of your arms around me
but you are nowhere in sight

I wish I had a magic power
then I would turn the hands of time
to change four weeks into one hour
and then forever to be thine

But the only magic which I own
is all my love for you alone

51. So Alone - Away From Home

So far away - away from home
so lost, so sad and all alone
my days are dark - my nights are sombre
that I've not lost my mind - it is a wonder

Oh how I bemoan my dreary fate
why have I come here, I think often of late.
I knew it be boring and lonesome some day
but to die broken hearted I thought not be my way

I wish to return as best possible now
to be safe in your love - make it happen somehow.
How can I be happy when there 's darkness around
when lonely and longing to these walls I am bound

As my heart breaks to pieces and the wind chills my bone
my life slowly settles to listless monotone
but my time will come when I can get up and go
and I'll never come back - not again suffer so

I know somehow I'll make it, somehow I'll prevail
for I'm a survivor, I succeed - never fail
soon I'll leave all behind and finally go home
where among all my friends I will happily roam

Where darkness and night are full of romance
where sadness and tears do not get any chance
where my days filled with laughter, my nights with love true
that's where I belong - heart, body and soul forever with you.

52. *The Other Woman*

There is a shadow in my life
which haunts me night and day
it's the woman to whom you are bound
and I know that she won't go away

53. *More Than Love*

Through darkness I had walked
without your hand as guide
now that your love is in my life
I walk into the light

With you there is a whole new world
which just in dreams I knew before
your tender loving ways each day
have touched my inner core

54. *Not Without You*

Today I've told you "it's over"
I asked you "please go away"
but I know that forever I need you and love you
and in my heart I had asked you to stay

I searched for a dream - I found it
and it became reality
but I could not hold on, no matter how hard I tried
fate took my dream away from me

Now that I lay down for all eternity
I will again find my dream
and I will live that cherished dream
that forever will live within me

You are my dream
without you I can't be
but when I wake I'm so afraid
what will become of you and me

I cannot live without you
and don't know if I can live with you
I guess the best fate for me would be death
and eternally our love would be true.

55. *Realization and Defeat*

Dreams we made
so fast forgotten
a love we shared
so ill begotten

Words can be the cruelest weapon
cutting like a well honed knife
but through a twist of fate you're dying
your heart is dead yet you're alive

Alone within a crowd of many
but no one ever sees my pain
the tears I cry while in my sorrow
the broken heart - it's all so plain

Yesterday was full of laughter
today is full of endless sorrow
and while I wish for a happy future
I'll only know a sad tomorrow

Atlast the greatest prize I found
I finally have lost
and all the smiles we shared, I bought
at much too high a cost

56. *Power Game*

You were the man I knew I wanted
the one who made me feel complete
I gave my love, pride, soul and honor
and you had filled my every need

I gave my all without a question
I trusted you without a doubt
believed in you and in our future
for that's what I thought love's about

But you would not give quite so freely
for you my all was not enough
you second guessed my every action
you didn't trust in honest love

Infinite power you were given
to hurt or love me at your will
you could keep me when it pleased you
or leave me when you had your fill

There has been but one choice for me
and this I know you knew
no matter how you treated me
I would come back to you

This game 's been played now once too many
you will not hurt me one more time
I'm taking back my independence
and once again my heart is mine

This does not mean I have stopped loving
but am resisting every way.
It is a slow and painful progress
but it leads to success one day

7. When I Need You

My darling, when you left me I was in despair
you said that I drive you away
I did really need you and wanted you there
but you turned, you did not want to stay

You don't understand that I need you most
when I'm down and can't get up on my own
but that's when you tell me depressions are games
you then have no patience or comfort to give
you turn and leave me alone

Could I turn back the hands of time
I'd do it right away
turn long-ago's into tommorows
and yesterday into today

I would undo the things done wrongly
turn back and go a different way
I would recall words spoken hasty
and say the things I didn't say

To live again all my decisions
to do right where I've done wrong
be more persistent where I gave up
do stay, not leave where I belong

How many things known, would be different
how many wrongs would have been right
how many hearts would not be broken
how many tears never been cried

Oh, fate, I wish that I could choose you
to live by my own plans and dreams
yet the path we take has long been chosen
we are but pawns in life's great sceens

Our future has been long selected
that's why all is as designed
if really given chance to change it
all I would change would be my mind

9. Time

Time's just like water through a sifter
nothing ever stops it's flow
you barely noticed you've arrived
but realize that you have to go

Time - never ending seconds
and minutes feel just like a day
it goes too slow while you are waiting
for one you love, who went away

Before all started - time was there
and when all's finished - time goes on
some measures time in years and eons
some count the shadows - short and long

We ourselves are but time measures
to start with birth and end with death
time can't be changed, nore stopped or altered
there won't be more - there'll be no less

Some measure time by their achievements
some just enjoy, let time go by
no moment ever gets repeated
time's old - time's young - time does not die.

60. *Materialistic Loneliness*

I drive a fast car
have two homes of my own
have credit cards and money
never will need a loan
but every night that I go to sleep
alone in my bed I lie there and weep

I can travel the world
it's far places I've seen
fine dining I enjoy
five-star restaurants I've been
but wherever I go no arms are waiting for me
to be unwanted and lonely is the prize to be free

I own diamonds and rubies
and emeralds and more
have more clothes that I need
shoes, boots, sandles, gallore
these are all fancy trappings which I'm wearing outside
a woman desperate to be loved - is what they hide

1. *On the Brink*

Within the palm - and pine tree's gentle swaying
the turquoise ocean it's waves
a calming rumbling song
he scent of tropic flowers lacing the salt mist air

I am a woman abused afraid and lonely
on an exotic island without someone to care
the night is black and shiny like a raven's wing in rain
the ocean's sounds and salt mist are beckoning me outside

Alone I walk the beach, behind I leave
my barefoot prints to marr the flawless, powdery, white sand
the deep and endless dark sea calls my name
it's star reflecting waves seem like death's beckoning hand

Shall I just mindless follow the secret calling that promises oblivion
and drown my torment heart within the ebb and flow
or shall I run and fight the icy fingers
that claw and wrap around my soul

I know within my tortured mind
death is the only way to ease the pain
and yet there is a rainbow following each rain
and given time to heal even the deepest pain will go

Set Him Free

Wise people long have set a rule
for lover such as me
that if you want to keep your dream
you have to set him free

Too many times I lost a love
for I went much too fast
I did not keep the "old one's " rule
and forced love cannot last

I'm on the love path once again
and if I brake this rule
I'll loose whatever he might feel
I'd be the greatest fool

I'll gladly give without return
my body, heart and soul
to never ask him or demand
just friendship and caring my goal

I'll be there for him whenever he wants
let him seek me of his own free will
I'll be his companion, lover and friend
and just for his caring - with joy my heart would fill

Some day I pray that by letting him free
his heart would be reaching for mine
and if by his choice he'll return what I feel
our love truley will be divine

I'll go to bed to dream of him
and think of him by day
hop for the moments he'll spend with me
and my love find it's way

3. *Fool for Love*

Far across the endless ocean
where the azur sky meets turquoise blue
where white tipped waves are swiftly dancing
my soul has gone to search for you

When we had started our friendship
I knew that you would set the rules
my mind understood and did except it
but love turns wise men into fools

My love for you made me a bagger
gratefull take what you would spare
I do not dare to hope you'd love me
but pray and dream that you do care

Oh, how I long to hear your laughter
to see your smile, to hear your voice
yet you deny your arms and kisses
and to accept I have no choice

Foresake me not, my sweet beloved
do not reject the love I feel
I would belong to no one other
what's in my heart for you is real

64. *Reality, Lies and Friends*

Reality is nothing but the death of an illusion
the destruction of your favorite dreams
when you get robbed of the comfort of darkeness
you have to face reality where nothing is the way it seems

The sugar coated lies are easy to be swallowed
you willingly believe as long as it sounds good to do
but the real test comes when the pill is bitter
and someone cares enough to speak the truth to you

It is so easy for friends to share the happy times
but be aware of faces which laugh and smile all day
for smiles and friends are fading fast
when darkness falls and bad times head your way

Sometimes it's hard to spot the one true friend among all others
the false ones all will tell you what you want to hear
their pretty words and compliments do never hurt
but your real friend will remain when all the others
stab you in the back and disappear

True friends are a rare commodity
you can never have to few or to many
for when you really need one
you might find out you don't have any

5. *Bitter Sweet Love*

Love is not always painless
it's cruel and bitter sweet
for when you love you're vulnerable
your heart is primed to bleed

Love can saturate your mind
a plethora of emotions
circumpassing all you've known
older that time - deeper than oceans

You'll hurt the one you love, the most
but feel the same pain too
you need him more than life itself
and pray that he'll need you

You have to trust him without doubt
and take his word as bond
true love does neither lie nor cheat
love has a truth beyond

And after all the pain subsides
the feeling that remained
sweet peace and all fulfilling bliss
love's worthwhile to be gained

66. *Don't Change Me*

What was it that you fell in love with
what was it that attracted you
was it what you hoped I'd be
or all the things I used to do

I used to be a fearless woman
so independent and carefree
a freedomfighter full of adventure
an unbroken spirit, a dreamer is what I used to be

Our lives have changed - we have each other
and we're adjusting willingly
but if you change my very being
at the end I will no more be me

Your care for me touches me greatly
but, Darling, please, do trust in me
don't crush my dreams - burst all my bubbles
don't put a chain around my neck -
open the door and set me free

My loyalty is yours forever
my heart and trust and love's yours too
you never need to doubt if you're my only
this barefoot contessa belongs to you

7. *The Dreamer*

Let me tell you 'bout the dreamer
for they are a special kind
among all other people
no more unique you'd find

The dreamer does believe in dreams
and tries to make them true
he lives within his own dreamworld
and often called a fool by you

Dreamers are a trusting people
they believe in the good in all
they are bound to hurt uncounting times
but relentlessly get up when they fall

There is a child in every dreamer
full of laughter and play
but too sensitive and emotional
they cry at night and laugh by day

Dreamers believe in fairytales
make a wish on a shooting star
they live carefree for today only
and are accused that they never go far

The one thing a dreamer does need most
is to be loved and to love
his quest is perfect harmony
of affection he can't get enough

A dreamer might die in his search for love
for he can't rest until it is found
he is honest and giving, loving and kind
but his free spirit will never be bound

The rare and special kind of dreamers
are near extinct and dying fast
people are trying to change them and brake their spirit
and in harsh reality the dreamer can't last

How do I know about the dreamers
and why I am telling thee
so you can learn and understood this special kind
for you are loved by and living with a dreamer - ME!

68. Hopeless Maze

Aimless, speechless. sightless
loveless, lifeless - that's my fate
where are the days of songs and laughter
the warm embraces, kisses - there's just hate

Where are the tears that help me drown the pain
they used to come so easily to flood my totured mind
now I just wish for them to fill the emptiness within me
but there is just the hurt inside and no relief I find

So many angry words - constant echos in my memory
a slow persistant cold is seeping in my heart
there are a thousand pathes out of this ugly maze
but I don't know which one will lead me to the start

The night sky used to shine with brilliant stars
now casts it's angry shadows, the moon has gone from sight
I do not know why past and future cannot be the same
it all is over now, my life is due - turn out the light

9. *Some Day You'll Know*

I've had enough of your abuse
you've hurt me long enough
so I'm putting on my walking shoes
and walking out on love

I know that I've been true to you
but you chose to think me wrong
when you find out that I was right
I will be long time gone

You tried to hurt me all you could
gave me more pain than I have known
still I can't hate you - though I should
forever I'll remember the evil that you've shown

You say that I'm a "has been"
you're happy to be free
someday I hope you'll remember
that there was love between you and me

You always believed the worst of me
you had no faith or trust
I now think that our love was all one-sided
that all you felt was lust

You tried to brake my spirit
you loved to see me cry
I know you're evil incarnate
and that your love was just a lie

Maybe you'll think I'll miss you
you might hope you broke my heart
but I'm already over you
I'm stronger than you thought I'll be
and I found a new start

Someday you'll hurt as you've hurt me
and then you will remember
a pair of green eyes filled with tears
and my love for you so tender

70. *One Day in Time*

One day in time
I always shall remember
with special feelings in my heart
so full of love - so tender
when you were mine
I always will remember

One day in time
when I had felt your lips on mine
in gentle plunder - so divine
and my heart beat as wild as thunder
matching thine
I'll not forget that day in time

One day in time
your kiss was hot as smolding ember
your strong arms holding me - a shelter from the storm
I gave my love and did my heart surrender
for you were mine
I always will rememeber

One day in time
a stolen moment - never to return
but when I think of you - for your caress I'll yearn
to drink again the kisses from your lips as sweet as wine
and feel you wrapped around me
one more day in time

One day in time
I felt a total peace and harmony
you are the essence of ultimate, unequaled masculinity
when we had joined - the universe did open
with tenderness and passion - you made me thine
for just one day in time

One day in time
I knew that I felt ecstasy
a magic moment just for you and me
could I just feel your touch - look into your eyes for one more time
to just pretend that you are mine
and I'll remember you
for all eternal time

1. In My Heart

I gaze into the bright blue sky
it's daylight - there is not one star
I see your face - so close so clear
I hear your voice - I feel you near
Your're in my heart
you're never far

I hear the rumble of the waves
a melody of nature's song
I hear your voice - so loud and clear
I smell your scent - I feel you near
you're in my heart
where you belong

I smell the scent of fresh clean air
the fragrance of a summer rain
I smell your masculine pure scent
I feel you touch me - touch my hand
you're in my heart
where you remain

I feel the night wind's soft caress
a full moon is about to shine
I feel you gently touch me - reach for me
I taste your kiss - sweet ecstasy
you're in my heart
where you are mine

I taste the salt mist on my lips
the remnants of the ocean's spray
I see you, hear you, smell you, feel you
you're in my mind so real, so true
you're in my heart
where you will stay

Your path in life is taking you away
away from me, away so far away
I stay behind
my arms outstretched for your return
for your return I yearn
while far behind I stay

72. **Who am I ?**

Another day has turned to night
another night has met it's dawn
slowly the years are taking flight
my life is moving on

How many times have I layn waking
to count the stars up in the sky
how many times thought my heart braking
for love that grew - then had to die

Who am I now - who am I really?
who is this woman - who am I?
all through my life I've paid so dearly
for every dream - for every lie

Have I learned from my mistakes?
have I got harder 'round the core?
how many tears a heartache takes
I have not counted them before

A heart in search of gentle caring
a tortured soul in need of mending
dreams and hopes I hold for sharing
I seek a love that knows no ending